An Education Report
of the
United Nations Association
of the United States of America

TEXTBOOKS AND THE UNITED NATIONS

THE INTERNATIONAL SYSTEM AND WHAT AMERICAN STUDENTS LEARN ABOUT IT

By Gilbert T. Sewall
American Textbook Council

ISBN: 1-880632-61-6

Gilbert T. Sewall, author

Text design by Charlotte Staub
Cover design by Douglas Tait, Inc.

Contents

Foreword 5

Preface 7

Executive summary 9

Introduction 13

Questions and design 18

Why are textbooks significant? 19

Why is the United Nations an important topic? 22

Scope of United Nations-related content 24

What the textbooks tell us 32

Conclusions and recommendations 53

Bibliography: Textbooks reviewed 61

Foreword

The September 11 attacks and the counterterrorism campaign undertaken by the United States and other governments, with the help of the United Nations, have seized America's minds. These events have directed our attention beyond our borders to a world that most Americans had not fully comprehended or imagined because that larger, more troubled world did not seem to touch this country

We at the United Nations Association share the shock and grief at the horrific attacks on our country and its people, and we condemn the acts of terrorism that took so many innocent lives. But we also believe that out of the grief and horror has come a renewed sense of cooperation, not only among the American people but also among the nations of the world.

In recent months public interest in the United Nations and its activities has risen significantly. Teachers and students alike want to learn more about foreign policy and the international system, the world beyond the United States, and the role of the U.N. as prime mover in the global community. Even though polls indicate strong support in the United States for the U.N., knowledge of what the U.N. actually does and how it works is woefully lacking among Americans.

Textbooks are part of the problem. As a consequence of flawed instructional materials, many young people have a very limited understanding of an organization that has played an important role in shaping their world. Others, while possibly holding a favorable view of the U.N., cannot name or envision any U.N. activities or missions other than peacekeeping. Young people and adults alike are oblivious to the U.N.'s wide-reaching programs in all areas of human life.

Unfortunately, when essential information on how the international system works gets left out of textbooks, Americans are brought up with little awareness of the role of multilateral institutions in the advancement of democratic ideals and economic stability worldwide. They learn little about the role of the U.N. system in carrying out humanitarian work for citizens of the world who have not reaped the benefits of globalization.

What textbooks say about the U.N. needs thoughtful reappraisal if U.S. schools are going to educate leaders who are familiar with how the global system works. We hope that this independent study and critique of the subject, commissioned from the American Textbook Council, a private research center in New York City, will persuade those who establish the curricula, who produce the textbooks, and who select the instructional materials to adopt books that more adequately portray the U.N.'s increasing involvement in world affairs over the past half century.

American students need to know how the world works. They need to know about the broad reach of the U.N. system. American students need to learn about the U.N. role in keeping the peace, fighting poverty, protecting the environment, helping to save lives and societies following natural or man-made calamities, standing up for human rights, improving health and education, and building democracy. Students need to understand the values and principles on which the international system was founded. Informed by these, we believe, American students will be much better equipped to function in an increasingly interdependent world and to be better citizens of the United States and the world.

William H. Luers

William H. Luers
President and CEO, UNA-USA

Preface

Textbooks and the United Nations concluded at the time of the Terror in New York and Washington. Events then and now are having a dramatic impact on social studies content and they will undoubtedly continue to do so. World geography and history, world religions, political systems, the meaning of global interdependence, and the issue of global terrorism will no doubt assume a new significance in the high school curriculum.

At this critical time in the nation's history, it has been a privilege to consider the state of internationalism as it is reflected in textbooks and to appraise how the diversified U.N. system shapes the conditions and terms in numerous areas of human life.

American teachers and students cannot assume that global interdependence and transnational issues are not facts of the twenty-first century. American students need to learn how the world works. They should be under no illusions about the manifold global challenges that demand international action, international cooperation, partnerships, and collaboration. Nor should they be under any illusions about the territorial and cultural obstacles to such ends.

Looming larger than any other single aspect of the international system, the U.N. is of paramount concern to the nation and the world. Students may know a few buzzwords about taking a "global perspective." But what does that mean? The longer one studies the U.N., the more evident it becomes there is no such thing as a global perspective. The 189 member-states, numerous agencies, and commissions that constitute the U.N. at the beginning of the twenty-first century show no sign of harmonic convergence, and the clash of nations, regions, cultures, and civilizations —

alongside the effort to advance human welfare—remains part of the world picture today and tomorrow.

The United Nations depended on the vision of many postwar American internationalists. Three of them were John J. McCloy, Elliot L. Richardson, and Potter Stewart, all ardent friends of the U.N. Each was prescient in viewing the global consequences of World War II and the urgent need for cooperation in many areas of human life. Each was unswerving in his commitment to the advancement of liberal democracy and global welfare. Freedom and human dignity across nations and civilizations were of paramount importance to these sentinels. I dedicate the following report to their memory, their early contributions to the U.N. and the international system, and what they represent to American internationalism in the twenty-first century.

I thank the UNA for granting the Council autonomy to frame the problem and pursue the textbook review independently, yet giving me sage guidance on several points. I am indebted to Jeffrey Laurenti for his subtle knowledge of the international system, correcting misimpressions and sharpening my own line of thought. I thank Lucia Rodriguez for overseeing the project and Charlotte Staub for its design. I was helped by early remarks and observations from Tedd Levy and John Fonte. Once again, I am grateful to Stapley Emberling, Roger W. Smith, and Peter Cannon for their critical contributions in research and manuscript: without their insights, this report could not have taken shape as it did. Any deficiencies are my doing, not the UNA's or that of any of these remarkable individuals.

Gilbert T. Sewall

December 2001

Executive Summary

History and government textbooks provide basic sources of information about the United Nations' role in international relations, its programs and activities throughout the world today, what it stands for, and what it does. The international system and what American students learn about it is a timely and important matter, one underscored by globalization and new kinds of global conflict. Textbook publishers, editors, and consultants have no doubt become more concerned with the U.N. system's role in advancing international security and containing terrorism than they were in the past. As history and government textbooks can make more clear than they do at the present time, the U.N. remains an expression of democratic values forged by fifty years of tense geopolitical events. It embodies a vision of international cooperation that transcends domestic politics. As a unique transnational agency that intervenes in matters of global interest to stabilize and secure civil relations among nations, the U.N. acts as a worldwide foundation of order and human welfare.

The American Textbook Council examined the content of seventeen of the nation's most widely adopted history and government textbooks used in junior high schools and high schools. Several questions launched our inquiry and study. What are the essential issues that textbooks should cover? How do the textbooks stack up? What do they include? What do they omit? What thematic approach do they take, if any, to cover the subject? Variations in the books reviewed are considerable, with coverage of the U.N. and U.N.-related subject matter ranging from non-existent and mediocre to sound and even adroit.

Few textbooks describe and explicate historical episodes or social, economic, and political issues in sufficient depth, as is stated below. In many of the textbooks reviewed, lessons involving the U.N. are so brief and sketchy that teachers and students are likely to be confused by its history and gain next to no grasp of the international system or how it works on behalf of billions of people. Complicating matters, the intricacy of subject matter associated with the U.N. (e.g., international law, the World Trade Organization) may be age-inappropriate for all but the most mature high school student.

Educators disagree among themselves what subjects merit inclusion in standard high school social studies textbooks. While individuals can argue reasonably over social studies content and subject matter, what is vitally important is that when any textbook raises a U.N.-related issue that it not dismiss an extremely troubling and complex subject in a few words or a short paragraph.

The primary purpose of this report is to inform editors and publishers and to convey to them the subject in a fresh light, one designed to improve volumes that cover the U.N. and world affairs. A second goal is to help teachers and educators improve U.N.-related lessons and expand knowledge of the organization. The study concluded and recommended:

✳ *History textbooks should be constructed so that they are age-appropriate, engaging, and lucid.*

This may seem to be a too obvious point. But the study finds that in U.N.-related subject matter in the textbooks reviewed, these content features were simply not the case. Lessons about the U.N. should not be up in the clouds. They should be presented in such ways that eleven- and fifteen-year-olds can comprehend, appreciate, and digest. In order to under-stand the U.N., students need to begin with concrete facts. They need to know something about the functions of government and the international-ization of these functions. Lessons should not begin with arcane theories of globalization, international law, and human rights. Abstractions such as these are simply beyond the grasp of many students: better for textbooks to employ actual examples from history and case studies of world affairs that root the international system in particulars.

> ✲ *Exact terminology is of utmost importance. Honesty and balance are imperative. Textbooks should note what the U.N. cannot do, i.e., the limits of global cooperation and meliorative capacity.*

Textbooks should not offer unrealistic forecasts of the U.N.'s power to protect the environment, control nuclear weapons, abolish the narcotics trade, end terrorism and piracy, or cure plagues. Nor should they offer a view of the world that gives American students a complacent or rosy view of the future. Textbooks should not minimize tensions that can arise between American interests and the international community.

Textbooks should not hesitate to tell the truth. They should explain that part of the international community is interested in the diminution or destruction of American influence and power. If history and government textbooks raise the subjects of peacemaking and peacekeeping — and they do — they should explain that these U.N. roles are at once its highest pro-file and most controversial functions. The international system, nation building, and world security are issues of momentous concern that are unlikely to diminish soon in the public mind.

> ✲ *Teacher education in world geography, world religions, world polit-*

ical systems, and world economics is critical to the quality of instruction and learning about the international system and global education.

It is a worthy goal to help teachers learn more about international coordination and cooperation, not only so they can use instructional materials more dextrously but also so they themselves understand how the world works. But such reforms and programs go beyond the purview of this report.

✴ *The American Textbook Council urges the United Nations Association to take action to prepare or commission a set of five booklets or one single primer covering U.N. history, U.N. organization and system, the U.N. and peacekeeping, the U.N. and terrorism, and U.N. personalities.*

Introduction

In November 2000, at the request of the United Nations Association of the United States of America, the American Textbook Council undertook a review of the nation's most widely adopted United States history, world history, and American government textbooks. These are standard texts used by students in school districts across the country between the seventh and twelfth grades. They include well established titles in multiple editions (found widely in classrooms) and newer books that publishers have recently introduced into key states such as California and Texas (the textbooks of tomorrow).

The subject of this study is the United Nations, how textbooks present its origins, its history, its role in international relations, and its programs and activities throughout the world today. The primary purpose of this report is to inform editors and publishers and to convey to them the subject in a fresh light, one designed to improve volumes that cover the U.N. and world affairs. A second goal is to help teachers and educators improve U.N.-related lessons and expand knowledge of the organization.

The Council's principal finding and complaint: in many of the textbooks reviewed, lessons involving the U.N. are so brief and sketchy that teachers and students are likely to be confused by its history and gain next to no grasp of the international system or how it works on behalf of billions of people.

This review extends the Council's long-standing interest in the history of the nation's international relations, in the content of world history and civic education, and in improving social studies education. It brings to the United Nations Association a digest of textbook successes and failures. We consider a number of salient lesson points that are intended to sharpen coverage of this many-shaped subject. We weigh geopolitical changes, international disputes, and transnational initiatives centered in the U.N. that have shaped the world since 1945 and make it a safer place. We reflect on the mandates for economic progress and human rights contained in the U.N.'s charter. The UNA, it seems to us, has an opportunity to raise the quality of content on a topic that brings together major political, economic, and cultural issues with worldwide implications.

The Council is aware of differences among social studies educators and among the public as to what the U.N. is and what it should be. The report is an effort to bridge the liberal and conservative views of the organization and system; to acknowledge social studies and historical approaches to the subject; to balance the past and current affairs; and to provide insight about an international organization whose reach goes very far but that few Americans understand.

Educators and opinion leaders whom the Council interviewed early in the review provided images of the U.N. that do not square with what it is and what it does. Even individuals who consider themselves progressive described the U.N. as costly, inept, and bureaucratic, though many of them envisioned the U.N. as an instrument of "peace education" and "transnationalism." Moderates and conservatives typically described the U.N. as anti-American, pursuing policies and points of view that are consonant with the regimes of many Third World countries and supportive of left-wing social agendas. They wanted to know, for example, why UNESCO makes Guatemalan activist Rigoberta Menchu Tum a roving Goodwill Ambassador, if not to promote a revolutionary politics that most Americans fail to share or want.

During the course of the study, individuals who were consulted and interviewed registered distress that, for whatever reasons, the United States lost its seat on a U.N. human rights commission. A U.N.-sponsored world conference against racism in Durban, South Africa, was seen as a calculated effort to shame Israel and the United States. This conference offended many American observers, and by this estimation, it impaired the U.N.'s reputation domestically at a time when international cooperation and comity assume unprecedented urgency. Complicating matters, conservative organizations that appear inherently hostile to internationalism assign blame to the U.N. that it does not deserve and impute consequences (notably in family, religion, and sovereignty) that do not stand up to inspection.

Americans may welcome the concept of interdependence and support many kinds of global regulation. But among those interviewed, across the political spectrum, anxiety attended the prospect of international agencies and law that might trump the United States constitution. The U.N. is an organization of sovereign and independent states, not a world government, yet it has the image for being the very thing. This is a misapprehension, we believe, that all social studies instructional materials can and should quickly correct.[1]

Americans of all ages flatter themselves that they think globally and act locally. The reverse, we fear, is much closer to reality. Discerning observers of all political perspectives complain about widespread indifference among

---

1. The U.N. enjoys more support, reporting shows, than is often acknowledged by members of Congress and by so-called practitioners. Steven Kull and I.M. Destler conclude in *Misreading the Public* (Brookings, 1999) that practitioners failed to understand public sentiment. "The dominant view, especially among congressional interviewees, was that most Americans have a negative view toward the UN.... Polls, however, paint quite a different picture of a majority that strongly supports the UN and U.S. participation in it..." (59) "The dominant view among the practitioners we interviewed was that most Americans have a

Americans to world history and international events. (This assumption was the primum mobile of the global education movement ascendant in the 1980s.) Flashpoints in world affairs such as Taiwan, Kashmir, and Jordan do not capture the interest of the general voting public. Until recently, for many Americans, the Islamic world that stretches from Morocco to Indonesia seemed to be not much more than an indistinct and far-away shape on a world map.

While the United States has come to rely on the U.N. as an international force and system, the organization's scope and operations are not well known among American citizens. In contrast, the rest of the world views the U.N. and its related global agencies as very important. Few Americans understand that the U.N. is a system of related agencies that cover and coordinate at the international level what governments handle internally. Ignorance prevails about international politics and law, both its nature and its limits, a condition aggravated by the complexity and scope of the topics and theory therein. The challenges in front of the U.N. stem from national rivalries, historical enmities, deep religious conflict, and geographic and economic imbalances that no schoolbook can single-handedly elucidate.

Textbook deficiencies are rooted in matters more basic than content, researchers agree. For more than a decade, critics of instructional materials and textbooks[2] have faulted social studies textbooks for unclear con-

---

negative view of UN peacekeeping..." (ibid., 81) Polls show, again, according to the authors, that the majority of Americans supports the idea of U.N. peacekeeping. For all the negatives, the U.N. is considered by a great majority of voting Americans to be critically important in global affairs and an instrument of world peace, deserving of respect and goodwill.

2. These include numerous studies and reports by Isabel L. Beck, Paul Gagnon, James A. Laspina, Sandra Stotsky, Harriet Tyson, et al.

tent goals, assumed background knowledge, inadequate explanations, and sloppy presentations that may bear directly on the absence of interest and comprehension too often reported by teachers and students. Concepts and events often go unexplained, these researchers have concluded. Complex ideas are broken down by textbook editors in the name of "readability," but the text is not necessarily improved.

What the public and media call "dumbing down" is a qualitative matter at the heart of textbook improvement. Shallowness and sloppy presentation plague many of today's textbooks. *Mentioning* is the term that textbook researchers and critics employ to describe textbooks that contain names of institutions and organizations, people and the like. These textbooks, however, fail to explain in even a rudimentary way what these names are, what these institutions and organizations do, why these people, places, and things are significant. The elements of a well-constructed instructional text, key ingredients to historical understanding and all good writing, are missing.

The elements of a well-constructed instructional text are missing.

The difficulty of the material compounds the problem. Many U.N.-related topics are simply age-inappropriate, that is, too abstract or complex for a young classroom audience. International policies, institutional strains, and conflicting agendas for the future that dog the minds of experts, trained diplomats, and specialists in regional and international studies are sometimes best reserved for college classrooms and specialized courses where student maturity, knowledge, and interest are likely to converge, stimulating meaningful analysis and discussion about international organizations and the U.N.

Questions and design

This study identifies, describes, and appraises the value of U.N.-related topics that are covered in the nation's leading middle school and high school textbooks. Lesson plans (and scope and sequence) in elementary and secondary-level social studies reflect the content of state frameworks and standards. There has been heretofore no systematic book-by-book analysis of coverage of the U.N. in the nation's social studies textbooks. The findings below were developed, analyzed, and compiled by the American Textbook Council de novo.

The Council first conducted interviews with teachers, professors, and opinion leaders to gain their impressions of the U.N. It identified and examined seventeen leading textbooks in three major social studies fields: United States history, world history and cultures, and American government. Geography and low-level civics textbooks were excluded. For purposes of comparison, the nation's most prominent 1961 text, *Rise of the American Nation*, once known as Todd and Curti, was also reviewed and reconsidered. Two history textbooks initially considered for review were excluded because of front-list changes on account of mergers and acquisitions in school publishing. Editions reviewed are recent student editions, copyrighted between 1994 and 2001.

The linkage of text and instructional activities was one important technical concern: Are different types of primary sources included, either as a complete reference or in a meaningful excerpted passage? Do review questions and other end-of-chapter exercises support the material presented in the narrative? How successfully do photography, graphics, and maps clarify (for example) geography, technological development, and cross-cultural relationships? Format and instructional activities aside, historians, teachers, and foreign policy experts agree: content accuracy, thoroughness, and perspective are much more important than other aspects of a history or government text.

> ✳ *Is the information in the textbook accurate?*
> ✳ *What subjects are emphasized?*
> ✳ *What themes and patterns emerge?*

In the case of world history in particular, issues of emphasis, weight, balance, and inclusion loom very large, in part because of the subject's vast scope and the limited number of days and months in the school year, in part because of conflicting schools of thought about the subject.

Why are textbooks significant?

Textbooks are the foundation on which teachers create their lessons. They are the primary source of information for students in classrooms across the United States in history and in all other subjects. Textbooks are familiar, efficient, portable, and relatively cheap. In many or most classrooms they are the sole source of information about the subject for teachers and students alike. They provide an organized sequence of ideas and information. Textbooks structure teaching and learning. Textbooks are time savers, providing a prepackaged "delivery system" that helps conserve teachers' time and energy. "A history textbook should provide rich, detailed, sustained, and interwoven narrative, with the teacher building, selecting, and refining its fare in the form of activities, displays, composition, direct instruction, and links," says Robert Hagopian, an eighth-grade social studies teacher in California who observes that "detailed, sustained, and interwoven narrative" is getting lost in today's overambitious and overdecorated volumes.

Textbooks are frequently the sole source of information about the subject for both teacher and student. They provide an organized sequence of ideas and information. How texts are created, selected, and used does much to standardize what is taught and learned in elementary and secondary schools. Some teachers are misled by graphic design and adornments. A standard student textbook and teacher's annotated edition remain primary sources of most classroom teaching and learning. Despite inroads of electronic media, printed textbooks will undoubtedly remain classroom staples for years to come. Teachers who are unknowledgable about history tend to be overly respectful of these instructional materials. They often assume incorrectly that learned researchers and eminent historians labor carefully to produce canonical tomes.

As textbook deficiencies grow more universal, teachers have less choice.

Almost any organized, informed, and enthusiastic teacher can overcome a deficient textbook. But as textbook deficiencies grow more universal, teachers have less choice and must adjust to the instructional materials they are given to use. Most textbook purchasers want instructional programs delivered to them whole. They do not want to take the time — or feel that they do not have the expertise — to build a course of study and history program from scratch. Textbooks are constructed and written for teachers who face daily demands and responsibilities not conducive to original class planning.

History and government textbooks are unique mechanisms of civic education and agents of national identity. In spite of innumerable panels, commissions, reports, and declarations during the course of twenty years, what an "international perspective" on social studies and general education means remains unclear. The literature on global education is vast and of mixed quality.[3] The ERIC database, the broadest and best bibliographic reference guide to educational research and analysis in this area, includes over 2,000 entries for global education and U. N. each.[4] Elastic terms they are—global education, global perspectives, and global studies —that have meant different things to different educators for a long time. Much global education theory, resource material for teachers, and instructional plans for students developed from the late 1970s seem in the post-Cold War era to be dated and geopolitically naive, even though such material remains a staple of teacher workshops.

To what extent is the U.N. a "humanitarian" agency? The word "humanitarian" does not appear in the U.N. Charter, nor in the charters of the specialized agencies, and in any event does not cover much more than disaster relief. What the word actually means, textbooks fail to say. Of humanitarian activities and humanitarian aid, a scholar at the Foreign Policy Research Institute asks, given the generally unimpressive or discouraging experience of the United States with humanitarian intervention, why does the humanitarian and human rights lobby continue to argue and agitate for it? There are a number of positive political, ideological, and moral reasons, he answers, but "sheer ignorance should not be underestimated. In short, most advocates of humanitarian intervention simply do not know what they are talking about."[5]

---

3. John Fonte and Andre Ryerson, eds., *Education for America's Role in World Affairs* (University Press of America, 1994) contains ten essays of differing perspectives on global education as well as detailed annotated bibliographies.

4. Go to the search engine in *askeric.org.*

5. James Kurth, "Models of Humanitarian Intervention," Foreign Policy Research Institute, August 2001, revised in *Orbis,* Fall 2001, 569-578.

This is a profound criticism that should not be brushed off or ignored. In too many classrooms, teachers and students debate complex global issues and conflicts with extremely limited direct knowledge and experience. World peace and security are discussed with the vocabulary and in the spirit of a Hallmark get-well card. Naiveté and wishful thinking — a deep aversion to looking at the harsh realities of a discordant world and the enemies of liberal democracy — are the rule. Issues that involve the welfare of all humanity, including those incumbent on specialized agencies and elements of the U.N. system, remain shielded from view.

Why is the United Nations an important topic?

The U.N. arises from the Allied vision of postwar global development. It embodies Franklin D. Roosevelt's Four Freedoms — of speech, of worship, from want, and from fear — incorporated into the Atlantic Charter of 1941, freedoms restated by the 1945 United Nations Charter and the 1948 Universal Declaration of Human Rights. These ideals provided an optimistic or at least a rational view of the future, emphasizing global interdependence, economic and social progress, human rights and liberties. As principles of international order held by a vast majority of American citizens, embodied in fifty years of declarations and statements as to be structural and interstitial, these ideals are intertwined with American foreign policy and efforts at global cooperation. They sometimes exist at odds with national security and self-interest.

The U.N. is important because the work of its decision-making and implementing institutions is everywhere, often invisible, working behind the scenes, vitally important as an agent of order, protection, and (sometimes) human improvement. The U.N. and its related agencies have become nerve centers of international politics, organizing responses to political and economic crises, and holding states accountable for serious violations of such law. In a major transformation of international relations since 1945, the U.N. has been at the center of the growing field of international agreements and law, trying to govern everything from information transfer, trade access, and prescription drugs to nuclear terrorism and the conduct of war itself. (It should be a foregone conclusion that international trade rules, for example, are a more functional area of international law than rules regarding terrorism and the conduct of war.)

The notion of "international community" — a term now widely accepted as normal usage among foreign policy specialists, academics, and the media — represents a dramatic development of the past several decades. It implies that a political system capable of debating and voting on expressions of the will of this international community is possible and to be desired. The elements of the international community include non-government organizations such as the Red Cross and Amnesty International, as well as regional intergovernmental organizations such as the European Union and African Union.

The manner in which the U.N. organizes responses to political and economic crises, how it monitors and reacts to violations of international law, and how it exerts collective pressure on nations are foundational to understanding world affairs and

> The U.N. and its related agencies have become nerve centers of international politics.

evolving protocols between nations in the twenty-first century. Americans may have good reason to be apprehensive about the development of international agencies with certain powers and resources to intervene in conflicts or in economic upheavals, the growing development of an international political system in which "citizens' movements" participate directly, and the blurring of frontiers and currencies.

Some authorities and practitioners, ardent supporters of globalism, maintain that individual states should be held accountable to the international community for violations of the standards that community has enshrined in international law. These cross-national extensions are not only matters of infinite complexity. Concessions to external authorities whose interests conflict with the United States and its allies are politically unlikely in the near future. In approaching the U.N., educators and students should ask: In what areas of human life and the life of nations is international law appropriate and practical? What are the limits of international law in light of police power and the capability of enforcement? How does international law square with nations that reject liberal democracy and market capitalism, especially on the European and American models?

Scope of United Nations-related content

The American Textbook Council identified U.N.-related themes, considering organizational, historical, and issues-related lesson points deemed significant and consequential by several well-regarded college-level histories of the United States and the world.[6] Secondly, the study took into account prescribed coverage of the U.N. in social studies and history frameworks and state standards published by California (1987 ff.), Virginia (1995 ff.), and Massachusetts (1997 ff.). A framework of history

---

6. Bailey, *The American Pageant*; Blum, *The National Experience*; Kagan, *The Western Heritage*; McKay, *A History of World Societies*.

essentials for high school students developed by Paul Gagnon in 2001 for the Middle States Council for the Social Studies, an affiliate of the National Council for the Social Studies, highlights the United Nations in the context of world affairs since 1945 and the Cold War. Gagnon's U.N.-related lesson points are: "the League of Nations revised; early American leadership; Universal Declaration of Human Rights; peacekeeping efforts won and lost." This lesson outline buttresses a larger unit in Gagnon's framework with lesson points on the Cold War in Asia and proxy wars in Africa and Central America.[7] At no time did the review expect any single textbook to include the panorama of subjects below. In fact, we reiterate, depth of coverage—not mere inclusion—was the best guarantee of a successful lesson.

The following enumeration gives a sense of the U.N.'s range and significance. It is designed to stimulate more thorough and imaginative textbook coverage of the U.N. — and remind educators and publishers of the range of the subject.

The five U.N.-related lesson topics that history textbooks are most likely to cover are based on index surveys. These lessons are subjects of widely acknowledged significance in global history and international relations since 1945:

★ *Creation of Israel (1947-49): U.N. partition plan. End of British mandate and Palestine-Israel War. Admission of Israel to U.N.*

★ *China and Korea (1949-53): Postwar conflict among the former World War II Allies inside Security Council. Rise of Communist*

---

7. Paul Gagnon, "Essential History Content for K-12," in David Warren Saxe, ed., *Middle States Council on the Social Studies 2001 Yearbook*, 60.

China. North Korean invasion. U.N. response and force. Resolution.

✳ *Cold War (1945-1991): Geopolitical competition between the United States and Soviet Union inside and outside the U.N.*

✳ *Persian Gulf (1990-1991): Politics of oil. Role of Iraq. Invasion of Kuwait. U.N. military action.*

✳ *Yugoslavia (1992 ff.): Historical-religious conflict between Muslims, Roman Catholics, and Eastern Orthodox. Ethnic intolerance and fanaticism. U.N. "peacekeeping."*

History and government textbooks alike often — but not necessarily — begin with the concept, the organization, and the functions of the U.N., moving the subject through a historical framework that may or may not include the work of U.N. specialized agencies. Do textbooks explain:

✳ *The idea of arbitration to settle international grievances and moderate international conflicts is a historically recent (i.e., nineteenth century) diplomatic invention? How do mediation, quiet diplomacy in a world forum, and fact-finding contribute to global stability and security?*

✳ *What is meant by "Wilsonian idealism" and "internationalism"? What are the reasons for the failure of the League of Nations? In what ways was the United States responsible for its failure? (These three questions set the stage for all further inquiry into the origins and purpose of the U.N.)*

✳ *The Allied (and notably American) desire during World War II to stabilize international relations and secure peace in ways that the League of Nations did not, to promote global cooperation? Do textbooks note fundamental improvements that were made in the U.N. Charter compared to the League of Nations, e.g., legally binding military force and sanctions, economic and monetary reform?*

✱ *The United States, Soviet Union, Great Britain, France, and China called themselves the Allies and these Allies created the United Nations? How each of these nations have a special role in the U.N. Security Council? How the role and representation of China loom particularly large?*

✱ *The special significance of the Security Council, which has primary responsibility for maintaining international peace and security? (For example, the Security Council oversees the international tribunals on Yugoslavia and Rwanda war crimes, inspections in Iraq, and U.N. peacekeeping forces.)*

✱ *The Security Council has the power to back up its declarations with force — though this power is effectively limited by the will of its member states? How is enforcement of policy restricted on account of the limited powers that sovereign states have entrusted to the U.N. and its related agencies? What indeed are the limits of global cooperation and meliorative capacity?*

✱ *The General Assembly is the main deliberative body of the U.N., made up of many more nations than the 51 that founded the organization? Why there are 189 members of the General Assembly today in contrast to the founding 51 nations and how the U.N. has assisted nations as they have struggled to become sovereign states?*

✱ *The doctrine of ethnic self-determination and anti-imperialistic sentiment, among colonizers and colonized, before 1945? How nation-states created in the 1940s and 1950s deal with difficult and sometimes irresolvable tribal, ethnic, religious, and territorial issues that strain the concept of self-government?*

Compelling non-historical lessons and study questions that elaborate the nature and role of the U.N. system and the international community include:

✱ *What is a non-governmental organization (NGO)? What are the advantages and disadvantages of an NGO standing in relation to nation-states and national governments, each with distinct (and often conflicting) interests? What do "nationalism" and "transnationalism" mean? What does "international community" mean?*

✳ *What are major U.N. initiatives to improve nutrition, protect water purity and supply, and encourage sanitation, vaccination, and immunization? What is the U.N. response to pandemic viruses, including ebola and AIDS? What about world population and population control, a subject of far reaching importance that frightens controversy-shy educators and that textbook publishers avoid out of commercial self-interest?*

✳ *How does the U.N. work to protect, house, feed, repatriate, and resettle millions of internally displaced persons and refugees who have been forced to flee their homes and countries? If textbooks raise this topic, they have an obligation to explain what is meant by such terms as "internally displaced," "civil war," and "ethnic conflict" as they apply beyond the United States' borders. Can textbooks even convey the stark realities of refugee settlements and the convoluted situations behind them?*

Then there are specialized U.N. agencies and some study questions that present themselves to teachers and students looking for issues in contemporary global affairs:

✳ *Food and Agriculture Organization (FAO): What is the relationship between the FAO and the so-called Green Revolution? Why is the Green Revolution one of the most significant global developments of the last fifty years?*

✳ *International Civil Aviation Association: How do nations set international air safety standards and rules of the air?*

* *International Monetary Fund (IMF) and World Bank: How does the IMF differ from the World Bank? How does one agency deal with infrastructural development and capital formation, the other with balances of payment and currency? How do the world's banking powers, especially the United States, enter into policy and management of each?*

* *World Health Organization (WHO): Do textbooks tell the WHO story of global efforts to control malaria? What is malaria and why is it a global affliction? In light of Harvard University economic historian David S. Landes' observations in his 1998 book,* The Wealth and Poverty of Nations, *tropical diseases, parasites, global scourges, and public health menaces are subjects of vital public interest that bear on socio-economic vitality, life expectancy, and the future of human life around the world. How do the WHO-sponsored eradication of small-pox worldwide and the issue of bio-terrorism fall within the scope of public health?*

* *The World Trade Organization (WTO), an international agency that is organizationally linked to the U.N. system, is the target of anti-capitalists, anarchists, and others who seek to destroy it. Why is the WTO such a global lightening rod?*

The self-declared locus of international law is the International Court of Justice (World Court):

* *How does the World Court decide legal disputes between countries? In what legal realms has the World Court made the greatest strides? To what extent (if at all) do countries agree to accept its jurisdiction? What is its jurisdiction? Where is the police power? What means exist to enforce rulings? What are the consequences of the international movement to try individuals for war crimes before international tribunals and states that claim the right to try citizens of other countries?*

And finally, intriguing questions arise about systemic world-scale coordination:

✳ *What is the kindred relationship among the hundreds of components in the U.N. system? To what degree are U.N. agencies autonomous?*[8]

Regarding the U.N. and globalization, international politics and world affairs, educators and publishers should consider a final point. Do lessons on U.N. structure and organization make clear that each specialized agency within the U.N. system has its own governing assembly of member states, tied in to different ministries in the capitals of those member states (e.g., health ministries to WHO, agriculture ministries to FAO, education ministries to UNESCO)? Do textbooks make it clear that the Secretariat — the operating arm of the General Assembly — has little or no effective control over specialized agencies and their budgets, the selection of executive heads, and policy? The World Bank and IMF, for example, have a different system of voting from some other agencies, one based on wealth. This gives a handful of wealthy countries led by the United States effective control over their policies. This style of control bears comparison to UNESCO, in the hands of a different school of thought about the economic, political, and cultural future of the world.

The answer is no, but to be fair, textbooks cannot make the room to do so, unless they choose to highlight some particular aspect of the U.N. in a special unit or sidebar (an obvious candidate for the future: the subject of terrorism). Nor should standard social studies textbooks be expected to do so, given the scope and sequence—i.e., the many other obligations—of the subject.

---

8. Under the chairmanship of the Secretary-General, the ACC (Administrative Committee on Coordination) brings together but does not oversee the executive heads of 25 major specialized agencies in the U.N. system.

Textbooks Reviewed

UNITED STATES HISTORY

PUBLISHER	FIRST AUTHOR	ABRIDGED TITLE
Glencoe	Appleby	*The American Journey*
Holt	Boyer	*The American Nation*
Prentice Hall	Boorstin	*A History of the United States*
Prentice Hall	Cayton	*Pathways to the Present*
McDougal Littell	Danzer	*The Americans*
Prentice Hall	Davidson	*The American Nation*
Glencoe	Nash	*American Odyssey*

WORLD HISTORY AND CULTURES

PUBLISHER	FIRST AUTHOR	ABRIDGED TITLE
McDougal Littell	Beck	*Patterns of Interaction*
Prentice Hall	Ellis	*Connections to Today*
Glencoe	Farah	*The Human Experience*
Glencoe	Greenblatt	*Human Heritage*
Holt	Hanes	*Continuity and Change*
Houghton Mifflin	Nash	*To See a World*
Holt	n. a.	*People and Nations*

AMERICAN GOVERNMENT

PUBLISHER	FIRST AUTHOR	ABRIDGED TITLE
Prentice Hall	McClenaghan	*Magruder's American Government*
Glencoe	Turner	*American Government*
Houghton Mifflin	Wilson	*American Government*

What the textbooks tell us

Coverage of the U.N.'s origins and originating global vision was more substantial, coherent and clear in United States history textbooks published 40 years ago. There are several reasons for this. First of all, there was much less U.N.-related material to cover. Secondly, four decades ago, history textbooks pitched narrative and literary level of history textbooks higher than publishers can or want to today. Thirdly, political history and international relations had a higher profile in United States history textbooks and curricula.

In the 1961 edition of *Rise of the American Nation*, known to generations as Todd and Curti,[9] the U.N.'s original purpose and aims are constructed through the Atlantic Charter, Dumbarton Oaks Conference, Yalta, and San Francisco Conference. Thus a student will learn about the disagreements as early as 1944 between the Soviet Union's ambassador, Andrei Gromyko, and the United States over Soviet representation, and disputes over the strength of the Security Council's veto power from the beginning. Todd and Curti explains what the Security Council, General Assembly, International Court of Justice, and Secretariat were designed to do. Then it moves on to include Secretary-General Trygve H. Lie's 1948 warning that the "intense conflict" between the East and West, that is, the United States and the Soviet Union, endangered the world situation.

Unfortunately, Todd and Curti coined what has become a textbook cliché, that the U.N. is an international town meeting, a canard repeated in several books to the present day. This is repeated, for example, in *Patterns*

9. Lewis Todd and Merle Curti, *Rise of the American Nation*, Harcourt, Brace & World, 1961.

of Interaction: "The charter for the new peacekeeping organization established a large body called the General Assembly. This was like an international town meeting."[10] The town meeting image is also *Magruder's American Government's* formulation: "The General Assembly has been called 'the town meeting of the world.'"[11] This rustic metaphor belies a unique American provincialism. In fact the U.N. calls itself a parliament of nations, a more difficult concept for students to digest, but one that raises an all-important point about the difference between a town meeting and a parliament and an international forum.

> **Todd and Curti coined what has become a textbook cliché, that the U.N. is an international town meeting.**

It is generally thought that the most widely adopted eighth-grade United States history textbook in the country today is *The American Nation*, authored by James W. Davidson. It is also the least instructionally sound and most content-challenged of middle-grade major histories.[12] This influential textbook covers the U.N.'s foundation in four sweeping paragraphs that are likely to sow student boredom and confusion rather than understanding:

> Many of the disputes in the Cold War were debated in a new international peacekeeping organization, known as the United Nations (UN). The UN came into being in October 1945, when 51 original members ratified its charter.
>
> Under the United Nations charter, member nations agreed to bring

---

10. Beck, 855.

11. McClenaghan, 451.

12. See Gilbert T. Sewall, "A New Generation of History Textbooks," *Society*, November-December 1998.

---

disputes before the UN for peaceful settlement. Every member had a seat in the General Assembly, where problems could be discussed. A smaller Security Council conferred on conflicts that threatened the peace.

Over the years, the UN's great successes have been in fighting hunger and disease and improving education. United Nations health officers have vaccinated millions of children. UN relief programs have provided tons of food, clothing, and medicine to victims of disaster.

Preventing wars has proved more difficult. Sometimes, nations have refused to go along with United Nations decisions. In other cases, UN negotiations or troops have kept crises from becoming full-scale wars. As you will read, the UN played an active part in the Korean War.[13]

This passage is tone deaf and flimsy. *The American Nation*'s subsequent lesson on the Cold War provides a notable case of confusion and outright inaccuracy. The Soviet premier Nikita Khrushchev appears at the U.N., banging his shoe in front of the General Assembly and world. But a year earlier than he actually did.

In September 1959, Soviet premier Nikita Khrushchev arrived in New York. He had come to address the United Nations. At first, Khrushchev spoke calmly, expressing hopes that the Cold War between the United States and the Soviet Union would end. Soon, however, Khrushchev's manner changed. Twice, he became so angry that he took off his shoe and pounded it on the table.

Khrushchev's visit symbolized the calms and storms of the continuing Cold War. As the two superpowers confronted each other, the nations of Africa, Asia, and Latin America became battlegrounds in the struggle.[14]

---

13. Davidson, 769.
14. Ibid., 776.

The inaccuracy — which is particularly troubling both in light of the fast-paced movements of United States-Soviet confrontations at the time, and the failure to mention the crucial U-2 incident on May 1, 1960 — is compounded by the failed effort to tell the story: an incident that could make history come alive for an eighth grader. The passage manages instead to make a telling detail in history meaningless. Later, *The American Nation* raises the issue of apartheid inexactly within the context of the spread of freedom in the post-Cold War world.

> In 1948, the government of South Africa began enforcing a policy of apartheid (uh PAHR tayt), or strict separation of races. The nation's non-white majority was segregated and allowed no voice in the government.

> In 1986, Congress approved economic sanctions against South Africa. The law forbade American companies to invest in South Africa or import South African products. The United Nations also pressured South Africa to end apartheid.[15]

This singular and unadorned declaration fails to explain why the U.N. pressured South Africa, what forms it took, or how effective this pressure was. U.N. involvement and the concept of pressure from the international community are rendered meaningless; the passage fails to convey the fact that the United States Congress was responding to a worldwide campaign for sanctions orchestrated by the U.N. This is a United States history, not a world history textbook whose scope might be expected to discuss South Africa's past in greater detail. But no history textbook— United States or world—should raise complex topics (in this case, racialism) unless it provides teachers and students with ample context and background.

---

15. Ibid., 835.

A second United States history textbook aimed at eighth graders, *The American Journey*, a volume that has been praised by several historians for its attention to American foreign policy and diplomatic history, introduces the U.N. in relation to the 1956 Suez crisis.

> Fighting did break out in the Middle East in 1956, when Egyptian president Gamal Abdel Nasser nationalized, or brought under government control, the Suez Canal from British control. Great Britain and France feared that Nasser might close the canal and cut off shipments of oil between the Middle East and Western Europe.
>
> In October, the two European powers invaded Egypt. Great Britain and France hoped to overthrow Nasser and seize the canal. Israel, angered by repeated Arab attacks along its borders, agreed to help by invading Egypt.
>
> The United States immediately sponsored a United Nations resolution calling for British and French withdrawal from Egypt. The Soviets threatened rocket attacks on British and French cities. In the face of this pressure, the three nations pulled out of Egypt. United Nations forces were sent to patrol the Egyptian-Israeli border.[16]

This is better history than *The American Nation*.[17] But why Suez? It is appropriate to ask why, of all the post-Korea and Cold War-related global events, crises, confrontations, and peacekeeping efforts in the 1950s and 1960s, the U.N. is introduced, fleetingly, in the 1956 Middle East crisis.

---

16. Appelby, 803.

17. But coverage of Suez in this textbook is sharply inferior to the succinct coverage of the event, the U.N. role, and its significance in geopolitics that is found, for example, in Todd and Curti, *Rise of the American Nation*, 805 ff.

Why, when many other U.N.-related historical events go unnoted? In regard to the entrance of the U.N. on the historical stage, a degree of arbitrariness is visible among many of the textbooks under review, a desire to include the U.N., but it does not matter much where. This is a relatively narrow criticism when *The American Journey* is compared to *The American Nation*.

In the early 1990s, Todd and Curti, in print from the 1950s, was remade into *Todd & Curti's The American Nation*, a textbook notable for its revisionism and splashy graphics that is widely used in high schools today. But coverage of the Korean War in the newer book is clear and complete. Curiously, the substantial U.N. role in the conflict, which the text explicates, is not to be found in the index. More recently, the U.N. appears as part of an undefined "new world order," and the textbooks review peacekeeping under the rubric of "Regional Conflicts" focusing (without good reason) on a program called Operation Restore Hope. A passage runs:

> In December 1992, United Nations forces, including many Americans, launched Operation Restore Hope to provide relief to famine-stricken Somalia. Fighting among rival clans in that country had prevented relief workers from getting food and other supplies to the starving Somali people.[18]

Two pages later, the book mentions U.N. failures in Somalia and Yugoslavia: "Although the United Nations sent peacekeeping forces to the area and launched an investigation into alleged war crimes of Serbian leaders, UN efforts did little to stop the fighting. In places such as Cambodia

---

18. Boyer, 960.

and El Salvador, however, UN peacekeepers played a more successful role." The statement reads in context:

> With the end of the Cold War, many hope that the United Nations will at last become the international force for peace that its planners had envisioned. By 1992, thousands of UN forces were serving on peacekeeping missions throughout the world. By 1993, however, the United Nations had compiled a mixed record in dealing with the most dangerous situations. UN forces in Somalia were not able to defeat the ill-equipped clans that were preventing relief efforts in that country. In Bosnia and Herzegovina, a former state of Yugoslavia, ethnic fighting among Serbs, Croatians, and Muslims left some 150,000 people dead or missing by the end of 1993. Although the United Nations sent peacekeeping forces to the area and launched an investigation into alleged war crimes of Serbian leaders, UN efforts seemed to do little to stop the fighting. In places such as Cambodia and El Salvador, however, UN peacekeepers played a more successful role.[19]

Such a treatment raises more questions than it answers. Some textbooks nearly disregard the U.N. *American Odyssey*, a history of the twentieth century, almost omitted the U.N. from earlier editions. The current edition describes events such as the Persian Gulf War, Yugoslavia, and South Africa, noting the role of the U.N. in each case.

Much more satisfactory United States history textbooks are available to high school teachers and students, however. At least two of them contain substantive and lucid coverage of the U.N. *A History of the United States* stands out. A strong and literate political history, it contains a thorough, blunt, and lucid account of the United Nations and the beginning of the Cold War.

---

19. Ibid., 962.

The fullness of *A History of the United States*'s U.N.-related narrative leaves other United States history textbooks far behind. Its description of the U.N. intervention in South Korea and the Chinese counterforce brims with precision and depth. Furthermore, this book, written by former Librarian of Congress Daniel Boorstin, explains the U.N. role in the creation of Israel and links it clearly to the 1956 Suez crisis. A U.N.-brokered withdrawal and the creation of a peacekeeping force, a U.N. resolution for withdrawal of Soviet troops from Hungary, the U.N. reaction to the Cuban Missile Crisis, and to Iraq's 1990 seizure of Kuwait, all of this is described clearly, even with a degree of polish.

A second widely adopted high school United States history textbook, *Pathways to the Present*, introduced in the late 1990s, considers the United Nations role in the Korean War and rasies the subject again in light of the establishment of Israel.

> Two years later, in 1948, the UN divided Palestine into an Arab state and a Jewish state. Zionist Jews had for years hoped to establish a Jewish nation in Palestine, but it was not until World War II, when thousands of European Jews immigrated to the region, that the Jewish population was large enough to form a new state. Tensions between Palestinian Jews and Arabs erupted with the UN announcement of the Jewish state, called Israel, on May 14, 1948. The United States and the Soviet Union immediately recognized Israel, but Israel was soon invaded by surrounding Arab states. Israel defeated those states and annexed most of the Palestinian territory, as shown on the map on page 732. While sympathetic to Israel, the United States tried to maintain ties with the oil-rich Arab nations of the region and to prevent them from falling into the Soviet orbit.[20]

20. Cayton, 731.

This well respected textbook slips in its treatment of recent United States foreign relations and interventions. *Pathways to the Present*'s treatment of the Gulf War is cursory:

> Working through the United Nations, the United States mobilized an alliance of 28 nations and struck at Iraq in January 1991 in "Operation Desert Storm." The Persian Gulf War lasted just 42 days. UN forces liberated Kuwait at the cost of just 240 soldiers, while tens of thousands of Iraqi troops died. Yet Hussein remained in power in Iraq.[21]

Pathways to the Present's brief notice of U.N. peacekeeping in Bosnia leaves even more to be desired: "The United Nations sent humanitarian aid and peacekeeping troops, but the fighting continued. Various peace plans were discussed and then abandoned." A subsequent passage on Somalia merely states: "President Bush sent American troops to assist a United Nations relief effort." The text goes on to say that "when several U.S. soldiers were killed in a battle with Somali rebels, some Americans demanded immediate withdrawal. Clinton recalled the troops later in 1993 without having restored order."[22] What is never explained is the U.N.'s and larger geopolitical interest in Somalia. Without context and elaboration, the passage is pointless.

World history is the most challenging area of the social studies curriculum, in part on account of its enormity, in part because of divided opinions among educators and curriculum specialists about its content. Two textbooks aimed at the middle grades present the subject of the U.N. with some care, but do so in different ways, one reflecting a "world cultures" approach, the other a "historical" approach.

---

21. Ibid., 951.
22. Ibid., 969-970.

To See A World, a world history and cultures textbook aimed at students in the sixth to eighth grades, contains a highly integrated teaching unit on the U.N., in contrast to other textbooks reviewed. This chapter, entitled "The United Nations, Israel, and South Korea," begins with a synopsis of the U.N. Historians may quarrel with the textbook's list of U.N. achievements (Bosnia, Somalia, WHO, and UNESCO), but they cannot fault the book's overview.[23] *To See A World* continues, "The history of two nations, Israel and South Korea, have been shaped by the actions of the United Nations." This overview is followed by a lesson on each country. The lesson entitled "Israel and the United Nations" is detailed, clearly laid out, supported by maps, and linked to Israel's situation and future. The lesson on South Korea, by comparison, is scattered and fails to explain the special relationship between the country and the U.N.

Human Heritage, a second textbook aimed at the middle-level world history classroom, does less with the U.N. "One result of World War II was the formation of the United Nations (UN), an organization like the League of Nations. In 1945, the United Nations was approved by 50 countries. UN responsibilities were to prevent war, lend money to poor countries, and provide them with medical care and better education,"[24] it declares. *Human Heritage* draws out the actions of the U.N. through an outstanding discourse on the Gulf War and a clear description of fighting in Bosnia.

> World history is the most challenging area of the social studies curriculum.

A world history textbook used in high schools, *Connections to Today*,

---

23. This is not an endorsement of the volume's overall quality: 1998 and 2000 American Textbook Council reviews note major flaws in other lessons.
24. Greenblatt, 621.

---

is the successor volume to *Patterns of Civilization*, a textbook that was prominent in classrooms through the 1980s and early 1990s. Not only has the made-over textbook become immensely more complicated—and confused. It reflects an effort to revise textbooks to stress current events and items of news interest, as well as such trendy topics as Third World poverty, the environment, and the advancement of women. They do not do these subjects justice, since these subjects are covered quickly and vaguely. By comparison, *People and Nations*, a long established high school world history textbook, is a more satisfactory volume, even though it does not linger on the subject of the U.N. It states succinctly: "In many ways the structure of the United Nations represented a compromise between those who still thought that great powers deserved more influence, and those who preferred a more idealistic approach to maintaining world peace on the basis of collective security."[25]

Connections to Today makes some valuable sallies into relevance, but a longish passage that purports to explain the U.N. does not:

> The United Nations was set up at the end of World War II as a forum for settling disputes. Its responsibilities, along with its membership, have expanded greatly since 1945. The UN played a vital role in decolonization. Since then, it has tried to act as a peacekeeper from Cambodia to the Middle East and from Africa to the Balkans. Some UN interventions have been successful. Others have failed, often because member nations could not agree on goals and methods.
>
> UN agencies provide services for millions of people worldwide. The World Health Organization (WHO), for example, helped wipe out

---

25. 755. The current edition of *People and Nations*, formerly authored by Mazour, and whose text remains close to Mazour in this edition, has no formal authorship attribution.

smallpox through its program of vaccinations. Today, WHO works with other groups to seek a solution to the AIDS crisis. Other UN programs aim to reduce malnutrition or ensure access to safe drinking water. The UN has also sponsored global summits, conferences of leaders and experts from around the world. These summits have discussed issues such as the environment, women, and population.[26]

These two paragraphs add up to a chaotic jumble. They refer to more than a dozen significant topics but taken individually or as an aggregate, they mean little or nothing. Individual educators will differ as to which of these topics, if any, deserve inclusion in the lesson. A tenth grader—who probably has next to no background knowledge about world health, environment, women's issues, or population—will remain in the dark. This passage fails to illuminate any of these issues.

Some subjects that textbooks raise are very difficult to render, as is indicated in a passage in *Patterns of Interaction*, one of the most extensive treatments of Cambodia found in the world history textbooks that were reviewed:

> In 1975, Communist rebels known as the Khmer Rouge set up a brutal Communist government under the leadership of Pol Pot. In a ruthless attempt to transform Cambodia into a rural society, Pol Pot's followers slaughtered 2 million people. This was almost one quarter of the nation's population. A Vietnamese invasion in 1978 overthrew the Khmer Rouge. The Vietnamese finally withdrew in 1989. In 1993, under the supervision of UN peacekeepers, Cambodia adopted a democratic constitution and held a free election. Pol Pot was captured and detained in 1997 for the war crimes he had committed.[27]

---

26. Ellis, 809.
27. Beck, 870.

In world history textbooks, coverage of African history and affairs was uniformly of very low quality. Thus, *Connections to Today* declares:

> After independence, African nations joined the United Nations. They contributed to and benefited from the UN and its many agencies. Africans served in UN peacekeeping missions around the world.
>
> African countries and other developing nations focused world attention on issues including health care, literacy, and economic development. They called for an end to racism and imperialism. They also pressed nations of the global North to deal with the unequal distribution of wealth.[28]

While each sentence is technically accurate, the text implies that U.N. peacekeeping is an especial African activity, and implies that Africa's role in the U.N. is the eradication of racism, imperialism, and unequal distribution of wealth.

This passage contradicts the book's following paragraph, which notes "famines and other crises," including starvation in Biafra, and that the U.N. fed "refugees of civil wars" in Burundi and Rwanda. It leaves blank the opportunity to come to terms with the realities of Africa. It does not dwell on the lack of arable land and navigable rivers, gross poverty, tropical disease or AIDS, tribal conflict or genocide. Of Somalia peacekeeping, *Connections to Today* says: "the UN and most foreigners withdrew, concluding that only Somalians could solve their own problems." What problems? The textbook gives no hint as to what went on, what was involved, and what went wrong in this peacekeeping venture. In

> **Coverage of African history and affairs was uniformly of very low quality.**

28. Ellis, 913.

an accompanying photograph on the same page, captioned "Turmoil and Survival," *Connections to Today* features women rebuilding their homes "after war in Rwanda forced them to abandon their villages," failing to mention the root causes of this effort. The page and lesson add up to less than nothing. *Connections to Today* states:

> The importance of global trade has been recognized by a series of international treaties. The General Agreement on Tariffs and Trade (GATT), signed in 1947, tried to establish fair trade policies for all nations. In 1995, more that 100 nations joined to form the World Trade Organization (WTO). Its goal was to establish global rules of trade "to ensure that trade flows as smoothly, predictably and freely as possible." Some people have opposed it.[29]

GATT and the WTO are very much in the turbulent center of global economic diplomacy today. (They construct and enforce global trade rules.) It will not do for *Connections to Today* to say merely that "Some people have opposed it," and let the matter drop, at a time when the hegemony of multinational capitalism is a matter that disturbs individuals of many different political views. Another book, *Continuity and Change*, also used in high schools, raises the issue of world trade, trade barriers, and globalization. It stakes out GATT and the WTO, but falls short when it loses the WTO somewhere between 1947 and the Uruguay Round:

> The scope of the 1947 General Agreement on Tariffs and Trade (GATT) was repeatedly enlarged in an ongoing series of negotiations among the major trading powers. In 1993 a seven-year round of GATT negotiations known as the Uruguay Round substantially lowered tariffs and

---

29. Ibid., 809.

protected ownership rights, such as patents, trademarks, and copyrights. It also led to the creation of the World Trade Organization (WTO), which had the power to resolve disputes between trading partners.[30]

A fourth high school textbook, *The Human Experience*, a book that generally covers world history with more finesse than competitive volumes, makes a pass at several important U.N.-related topics. It emphasizes human rights and the 1948 Universal Declaration of Human Rights. Unfortunately, it does not detail the content of this declaration, but notes it is "a statement not of the way things are, but of the way they should be." The U.N.'s role in Korea goes barely mentioned. The book mentions U.N. peacekeeping in the context of the Congo, Cambodia, and Bosnia, no more. In *The Human Experience*, U.N. peacekeeping is mentioned regarding the Congo: "UN peacekeeping forces arrived in Congo to prevent the superpowers from becoming involved. After settling differences, Katanga finally returned to Congolese rule, and UN forces withdrew in 1964." The section on Cambodia is extensive and more detailed than in many other world history volumes, but of the U.N., the book says only: "In October 1991, representatives of the four major political groups in Cambodia signed an agreement that ended the civil war and called for an election under U.N. peacekeepers," which does not tell the reader much at all.

Some history textbooks cover HIV, women's rights, and environmentalism as U.N.-related subjects. Whether or not the U.N. is the right context for these subjects is questionable. But it is evident that some social studies editors feel under pressure to adjust history textbooks to fit the moment and introduce new subjects popular with teachers and curriculum

---

30. Hanes, 848.

specialists. To do so, textbook marketers may add to the text an item such as the 1992 U.N.-sponsored Brazil conference on the environment or the 1995 Beijing women's conference. They are searching—often very hard—for material that will beef up history-related teaching units on new-paradigm topics such as environmental education or feminism.

World history textbooks may raise sensitive issues but do so in an utterly opaque way. For example, *Continuity and Change* states: "Efforts to protect the environment continued, however. In 1992 environmentalists convinced more than 150 nations attending a United Nations environmental conference in Brazil to sign a Convention on Biological Diversity. But the terms of the treaty were vague, and enforcement appeared difficult, if not impossible."[31] The critical environmental issues raised at the conference and international disputes that have ensued go unnoted. The passage is as vague as the treaty.

When social studies editors determine U.N.-related textbook content not on the basis of historically significant themes but because such a perspective fits into a new paradigm, they are also likely to stimulate distrust and even give the appearance of political propaganda. Such interpretations and thematic angles give the mistaken impression that the U.N.'s main mission is to advance controversial policies and agendas. Some topics such as racism, women's rights and roles in the non-Western world, and the environment arguably deserve inclusion in the curriculum, but not in the context of the U.N.

Such misrepresentation hurts the U.N. in the long run. More important from the standpoint of global studies and world affairs: Such a twist loses

31. Ibid., 843.

sight of the U.N.'s original vision and intent, its historical actions that affect the global present and future, and its raison d'être. This symbolic content drives to the side what U.N.-related lessons can teach, i.e., geopolitical relations, an evolving doctrine of human rights and freedom, and global economic interdependence.

American government textbooks are designed for eleventh and twelfth graders who as likely as not consider themselves college-bound. The most widely adopted textbook in this subject area is *Magruder's American Government*, which has been in print for some seven decades. *Magruder's American Government* deals with the U.N. in light of foreign policy and national defense. The book contains a useful précis of international relations from 1945 on. It stresses peace through collective security, and to that end, the book says the United States took the lead in creating the U.N. It states with refreshing bluntness: "It soon became clear that the future of the world would not be shaped in the U.N., however. Rather, international security would depend largely on the nature of the relations between the two superpowers, the United States and the Soviet Union. These relations, never very close, quickly deteriorated — and for the next 40 years American foreign policy was built around that fact."[32]

Magruder's American Government declares that because the U.N. did not immediately fulfill the dreams on which it was founded, the United States came to rely on regional security alliances. As do several other civics and government textbooks, *Magruder's American Government* outlines the principal organs of the U.N. Its historical summary of United States

---

32. McClenaghan, 443.

foreign policy is well-constructed and provides useful context for a following section on U.N. operations.

As do other American government textbooks, *Magruder's American Government* stresses the role of the Security Council and its effort to stabilize international relations through economic and military sanctions. It contends that the Security Council has undertaken a military operation only once in Korea. It says obliquely that the Security Council "has provided U.N. peacekeeping forces in several trouble spots." Unfortunately, a visually stunning table turns out to be nothing but a useless list of U.N. bodies, committees, specialized agencies, and subsidiaries.

> **Textbooks lose sight of the U.N.'s original vision and intent.**

Another government textbook used in classrooms across the country, *American Government: Principles and Practices*, covers the U.N.'s peacekeeping initiatives, by some lights, too critically or even incorrectly. The following passage reveals as well the difficulties of compressing contemporary events into meaningful narrative.

> Since the UN has no sovereignty, it cannot force members to abide by the UN Charter. UN members, for instance, have failed to agree on establishing a permanent police force to handle international disputes, and, as a result, the UN must rely on persuasion or temporary forces donated by member nations. UN troops were able to stop North Korean aggression against South Korea. More recently, however, they were unable to halt fighting between Christian and Islamic forces in Lebanon. In 1994, in Bosnia, the warring factions in the region openly scorned the UN forces that had been sent to restore peace. Serbian insurgents even took some peacekeeping forces hostage. In the face of

mounting hostility, the United Nations withdrew all forces from the wartorn land.[33]

The same book brings up an important and original point ignored by all other volumes that were reviewed:

> The United Nations also faces financial problems. Each UN member is responsible for paying a portion of the organization's operating expenses, with contributions based on a nation's ability to pay. Today, the United States pays the highest rate of any nation — 25 percent of the regular annual budget. Some smaller nations pay the minimum of 1/100 of 1 percent, and other nations' contributions fall somewhere in between. Russia, for instance, pays 6 percent. Compounding the problem is the failure of many nations to keep up with their payments. In addition, other nations have failed to pay special assessments for such operations as peacekeeping forces.[34]

It would be illuminating for *American Government: Principles and Practices* to state that one of the nations that have failed to keep up with U.N. payments is the United States and that the reasons have much to do with conflicting domestic schools of thought about foreign policy.

Peacekeeping is at least mentioned in most of the textbooks that were reviewed. The treatments vary, but in most cases, superficiality prevails. In the world history textbook *Patterns of Interaction*, the passage on peacekeeping activities is jumbled enough to make the reader wonder as to the point and value of inclusion:

> More than 180 nations send representatives to the U.N., which has as

---

33. Turner, 668.

34. Ibid.

one of its aims to promote world peace. The UN provides a public forum, private meeting places, and skilled mediators to help nations try to resolve conflicts at any stage of their development.

The UN also provides peacekeeping soldiers at the invitation of the warring parties. These forces try to prevent the outbreak of new fighting or to help enforce a cease-fire. The unarmed or lightly armed soldiers fire their weapons only in self-defense. The presence of neutral UN soldiers helps prevent aggression. In the late 20th century, the UN sent successful peacekeeping forces to such places as El Salvador in Central America, Kuwait in the Middle East, and Namibia in Africa. The UN, however, was only successful when the nations involved in a conflict maintained a commitment to working things out peacefully.[35]

Some treatments are hard to fault, given the limitations of textbooks as a genre. Compare the passage above to a compact passage on the U.N. and peacekeeping from another textbook, also titled *American Government*, widely used in honors and Advanced Placement courses:

> The United Nations has had a long history of efforts to settle conflicts between member nations. Between 1948 and 1993 it sent more than thirty missions to monitor cease-fire agreements, observe national elections to make sure they were fair, or provide security for humanitarian operations. Most of these missions involved small numbers of troops contributed by United Nations members. Before 1991 it was rare for either the Soviet Union or the United States to provide any of these peacekeeping forces; the antagonism between the two great powers made such cooperation almost impossible, and the presence of either one alone in a UN force would have undercut the UN's appearance of neutrality.

---

35. Beck, 952.

With the collapse of the Soviet Union and the end of the cold war, the United Nations is no longer dominated by the conflict between the United States and the Soviet Union. The United Nations' military effort in Kuwait was organized and largely controlled by the United States and was not opposed by Russia.

UN peacekeeping missions have also become more numerous. The UN played a role in sending troops that attempted to restore order in Somalia and that tried to protect humanitarian aid being shipped into what once was Yugoslavia. By 1993 United States troops were part of UN missions in seven different locations around the globe.

Some American leaders welcomed this development as the beginning of a new era in which the United States would use force in other parts of the world only, or chiefly, as part of a UN effort involving many nations. But other leaders worried that the United States, as the sole remaining military superpower, ought not to let its forces be directed by an international organization in which the United States had but one vote. The former leaders want the United States to work through the UN; the latter ones do not want to see United States policy controlled by other nations (many of which have dictatorial or hostile governments). As political conflict erupts around the globe with seemingly increasing frequency and intensity, the United States' relationship to the United Nations is likely to continue to be an important foreign policy issue. Liberals, especially those with a disengagement worldview, often want the United States to use military force abroad only as part of a United Nations effort. Conservatives, especially those with an antiappeasement worldview, tend to favor acting without United Nations authority or controls.[36]

---

36. Wilson, 627-628.

The variations in the seventeen history and government textbooks examined are considerable, with coverage of the U.N. and U.N.-related subject matter ranging from non-existent and mediocre to sound and even adroit.

Conclusions and recommendations

The almost reverential view of the U.N. among Americans that marked previous decades is matched by an overabundance of cynicism today. What the U.N. does, how it does what it does, the instruments it employs, and the obstacles it faces are matters of global importance. The subject requires a measured response to this domestic skepticism. Part of the project requires changes and improvement in social studies textbooks. The necessities of international cooperation in matters such as germ warfare and nuclear terrorism are compelling and unmistakable.

Social studies textbooks and the frameworks that determine their content have long cautioned against imperialism and unbridled nationalism, American or otherwise. Textbooks and curricula thus align with prevailing public opinion, the experience of the World Wars of the twentieth century, and massive efforts during the last fifty years to develop civil polities and functional economies throughout the world.

The United States and other leading nations have vested this effort in the U.N. and its related agencies. The inclusive study of the U.N., it is evident, will help the next generation of American voters and citizens gain a better understanding of how the world works and how nations' interests overlap.

United States histories, world histories, and American government textbooks, of course, have different subject obligations to the U.N. United

States history textbooks naturally present international affairs and organizations through the lens of American foreign policy after 1945. World histories and world cultures textbooks have more obligation to concentrate on geopolitics and global issues than do U.S. histories. In world history textbooks, compared to United States histories, for example, the Korean War obtains little space and consideration. In world cultures textbooks, apartheid may obtain more room than in other genres. Government textbooks may limit their discussion of the U.N. to broader, non-historical issues of U.N. organization, e.g., structure and collective security. They may be expected to outline the U.N.'s conceptual foundations, objectives, and responsibilities, including the organization's relationship to American foreign policy. In government books, historical context is helpful (and often available).

Structural problems of textbook shallowness amplify omissions.

As readers of this report should keep in mind, social studies textbooks are stretched to the breaking point. They are supersaturated with facts and factoids. They include a carnival of graphics and activities. History textbooks rarely afford detail on any subject. Practically speaking, it is important to keep in mind that textbook editors and publishers are reluctant to include additional content in over-packaged textbooks that already try to cover too many subjects and fall into the trap of repeated superficiality and unintelligibility. It is not productive to identify and enumerate items and themes — and then hope or assume that the U.N. will be studied in greater detail at the expense of other lesson points and content.

Structural problems of textbook shallowness amplify omissions. When the U.N. is involved in an episode or issue, the involvement rarely gets explained. Few textbooks describe and explicate historical episodes or social, economic and political issues in sufficient depth. Few give a solid idea of what the U.N. has been, is, and does.

Overall, American government textbooks cover the U.N. organization and its global role with greater clarity than United States and world history textbooks. Among individual textbooks reviewed, coverage of the U.N. varied substantially in content, emphasis, and interpretative finesse. In some history textbooks that were reviewed, the U.N. is virtually absent. Indexes were not entirely trustworthy. Some textbooks are more exactly indexed than others. Too frequently, U.N.-related events and issues are indexed, then mentioned on a jumbled page, no more. While the U.N. is cited or referred to, its role often remains mysterious. Among textbooks that we examined this lack of depth and cryptic narrative were more common than not. Some popular textbooks reviewed, not just *The American Nation* and *Connections to Today*, were deficient in content and worse in literary style.

U.N.-related subject matter most likely to be cited in history textbooks includes lesson points on Israel and the Mideast, Korea, the Persian Gulf, and the Balkans. Coverage of African affairs and the Cold War is spotty and uneven. The U.N.'s role in ending colonialism is rarely mentioned, much less covered with any acuity or insight. A hot war that was part of a cold war, Korea between 1950 and 1953 provides the study of U.N. military action at a time when the United States acted to lead the organization as a global police force. The Korean War was one of the signal events of the postwar era, history textbooks agree, part of the United States' postwar effort to contain and extirpate communism. On the other hand, history textbooks rarely mention or explicate the U.N. role in other Cold War events of acknowledged importance, e.g., Hungary (1956) and the Cuban Missile Crisis (1962).

Curriculum is about making choices. The American Textbook Council recognizes the difficulties in constructing any history-social studies program, given competing demand for thematic and content room. World history's enormous scope means that rich narratives on Haiti, Kosovo, East Timor, and Sierra Leone today — and detailed explanations to students why the U.N. takes special interest in these locations — are almost out of the question. (The basic geography of the Caribbean, Balkans, Indonesia, and West Africa would be a good place to start.) Since the U.N. is a global organization, its coverage fits with the trend toward world cultures courses at the middle-grade level, served to a degree by *To See a World* and *Human Heritage*.

Educators disagree among themselves as to what subjects merit inclusion in standard high school social studies textbooks. While individuals can argue reasonably over social studies content and subject matter, it is vitally important that any textbook raising a U.N.-related issue not dismiss an extremely troubling and complex subject in a few words or a sentence. History and government textbooks should make clearer than they now do that the U.N. remains an expression of the quest for global security forged by fifty years of tense geopolitical events. It embodies a vision of international cooperation that transcends domestic politics. As a unique transnational agency that intervenes in matters of global interest to stabilize and secure civil relations among nations, the U.N. acts as a worldwide foundation of order and human welfare.

✷ *History textbooks should be constructed so that they are age-appropriate, engaging, and lucid.*

Lessons about the U.N. should not be up in the clouds. They should be presented in such ways that eleven- and fifteen-year-olds can comprehend, appreciate, and digest. In order to understand the U.N., students need to begin with concrete facts. They need to know something about the functions of government and the internationalization of these functions. Lessons should not begin with arcane theories of globalization, international law, and human rights. Abstractions such as these are simply beyond the grasp of many students: better for textbooks to employ actual examples from history and case studies of world affairs that root the international system in particulars.

World histories should include lesson points that pose global perils, knowing in advance that these points can be highly controversial and even inflammatory. The protection of water and food? The threat of epidemic disease? How do the world's nations intend to create international standards for the Internet? Difficult questions before the U.N., how nations are to deal with nuclear weapons, biological warfare, piracy, smuggling, and terrorism, assume new and monumental importance inside and outside the curriculum.

✷ *Exact terminology is of utmost importance. Honesty and balance are imperative. Textbooks should note what the U.N. cannot do, i.e., the limits of global cooperation and meliorative capacity.*

Textbooks should not offer unrealistic forecasts of the U.N.'s power to protect the environment, control nuclear weapons, abolish the narcotics trade, end terrorism and piracy, or cure plagues. Nor should they offer a view of the world that gives American students a complacent or rosy view of the future. Textbooks should not minimize tensions that can arise between American interests and the international community.

Textbooks should not hesitate to tell the truth. They should explain that part of international community is interested in undermining U.S. influence and power. American teachers and students should not embrace the international community without knowing something about its composition and sources of authority. Textbooks should make a clear distinction between global cooperation and coordination, and between international activities that extend and complement national activities, and transnational activities that have ambitions to supersede nation-states. They should demand critical thinking about "world government" and "world citizenship."[37]

Textbooks should clarify what they mean when they use such terms as *international law, citizens' movements, "humanitarian" initiatives, peacekeeping, rogue states,* and *proxy wars.* It does no good to say only, for example, that "Special agencies carry out the humanitarian efforts of the United Nations. Humanitarian means having concern for and encouraging human welfare,"[38] and let the matter hang, as in *To See a World.*

---

37. Teachers and students might reflect on the warning of the political philosopher Hannah Arendt in her 1968 book, *Men in Dark Times*: "Nobody can be a citizen of the world as he is the citizen of his country .... The very notion of one sovereign force ruling the whole earth, holding the monopoly of all means of violence, unchecked and uncontrolled by other sovereign powers, is not only a forbidding nightmare of tyranny, it would be the end of all political life as we know it. Political concepts are based on plurality, diversity, and mutual limitations. A citizen is by definition a citizen among citizens of a country among countries.... Philosophy may conceive of the earth as the homeland of mankind and of one unwritten law, eternal and valid for all. Politics deals with men, nationals of many countries and heirs to many pasts; its laws are the positively established fences which hedge in, protect, and limit the space in which freedom is not a concept, but a living, political reality. The establishment of one sovereign world state, far from being the prerequisite for world citizenship, would be the end of all citizenship."

38. Nash, *To See a World*, 645.

If history or government textbooks raise the subject of human rights or the environment, for example, they should not flinch from the fact that many nations that belong to the U.N. have dismal records in human rights and the environment. American students must understand that various nations and individuals reject the American and European model of government and economic organization. They must understand that these nations represent a large bloc of the General Assembly, a forum that operates on democratic premises and principles.

  ✱ *If history and government textbooks raise the subjects of* peacemaking *and* peacekeeping—*and they do*—*they should explain that these U.N. roles are at once its highest profile and most controversial functions.*

Questions are not answered, leaving teachers and students to suppose that the U.N. appears as if by magic and brings peace to a place where there was formerly hate and bloodshed. Do textbooks explain the difference between U.N. "peacekeepers" inserted into an ongoing war and those who are sent to monitor an agreed peace? What are examples of each? What does peacekeeping entail, and what are good examples for textbooks to use? Where do U.N. soldiers come from? Who pays for them? Who commands them? How are they disciplined? How do they intervene to reduce hostilities and do so in a "limited" way? How does the U.N. engage in "nation-building" and what obstacles does the U.N. face in this process in anarchic regions of the world?

These are intriguing and important questions that college-bound twelfth graders can consider in educationally constructive ways. Terrorism —what it is, why it threatens all nations and global civilization, how it is manifest—has until now been a matter of minor textbook concern, an omission that textbook publishers will no doubt try to correct in short order.

Teacher education in world geography, world religions, world political systems, and world economics is critical to the quality of instruction and learning about the international system and global education. Helping teachers learn more about international coordination and cooperation, not only so they can use instructional materials more dextrously but also so they themselves understand how the world works, are ambitious aspirations. Such reforms and programs go beyond the purview of this report.

✱ *The American Textbook Council urges the United Nations Association to take action to produce for libraries and classrooms a set of five booklets or one single primer in which able historians and journalists collaborate to prepare episodic narratives and expositions of the U.N. in five specific areas: U.N. history, U.N. organization and system, U.N. peacekeeping, U.N. and terrorism, and U.N. personalities, that teachers can use as supplementary material to back up textbooks. These readings should elicit student interest through dramatic vignettes and vital personalities.*

Reading experts, historians and social scientists, journalists, and educational critics assert that absence of narrative and lack of context in the core text — less and less part of today's standard social studies textbook — override all other aspects of textbook deficiency. It is strongly recommended that any supplementary instructional materials that are developed to support textbooks and frameworks tell the story of the U.N. through compelling stories. They should include vivid biographies, for example, of U.N.-related figures such as Eleanor Roosevelt, Adlai Stevenson, Bernard Baruch, Ralph Bunche, Dag Hammarskjöld, Daniel Moynihan, George H. W. Bush, Andrew Young, and Jeane Kirkpatrick.

Bibliography: Textbooks reviewed

United States History textbooks aimed at 8th and 11th grades

Appleby, Joyce, Alan Brinkley, and James M. McPherson. *The American Journey*. Glencoe/McGraw-Hill, 1998.

Davidson, James West, Pedro Castillo, and Michael B. Stoff. *The American Nation*. Prentice Hall, 2000.

United States History textbooks aimed at 11th grade

Boorstin, Daniel J. and Brooks Mather Kelley, with Ruth Frankel Boorstin. *A History of the United States*. Prentice Hall, 2002.

Boyer, Paul. *Todd & Curti's The American Nation*. Holt, Rinehart and Winston/Harcourt Brace, 1995.

Cayton, Andrew, Elisabeth Israels Perry, and Allan M. Winkler. *America: Pathways to the Present*. Prentice Hall, 1998.

Danzer, Gerald A., J. Jorge Klor de Alva, Louis E. Wilson, and Nancy Woloch. *The Americans*. McDougal Littell/Houghton Mifflin, 1998.

Nash, Gary B. *American Odyssey: The United States in the 20th Century*. Glencoe/McGraw-Hill, 2002.

World History textbooks aimed at 7th to 9th grade

Greenblatt, Miriam and Peter S. Lemmo. *Human Heritage: A World History*. Glencoe/McGraw-Hill, 2001.

Nash, Gary B., Beverly J. Armento, J. Jorge Klor de Alva, Christopher L. Salter, Louis E. Wilson, and Karen K. Wixson. *To See a World: World Cultures and Geography*. Houghton Mifflin, 1994.

World History textbooks aimed at 10th to 12th grade

Beck, Roger B., Linda Black, Larry S. Krieger, Phillip C. Naylor, and Dahia Ibo Shabaka. *World History: Patterns of Interaction*. McDougal Littell/Houghton Mifflin, 1999.

Ellis, Elisabeth Gaynor and Anthony Esler. *World History: Connections to Today.* Prentice Hall, 2001.

Farah, Mounir A. and Andrea Berens Karls. *World History: The Human Experience.* Glencoe/McGraw-Hill, 1999.

Hanes, William Travis, III. *World History: Continuity and Change.* Holt, Rinehart and Winston/Harcourt Brace, 1999.

World History: People and Nations. Holt, Rinehart and Winston/Harcourt Brace, 2000.

American Government textbooks aimed at 10th to 12th grade

McClenaghan, William A. *Magruder's American Government.* Prentice Hall, 2000.

Turner, Mary Jane, Kenneth Switzer, and Charlotte Redden. *American Government: Principles and Practices.* Glencoe/McGraw-Hill, 1996.

Wilson, James Q. and John J. DiIulio, Jr. *American Government: Institutions and Policies*, Seventh Edition. Houghton Mifflin, 1998.